The World in One Square Mile

Central Falls

Stillwater River
Publications

Visit our website at www.StillwaterPress.com for more information.
First Stillwater River Publications Edition

ISBN: 1-946-30031-4
ISBN-13: 978-1-946-30031-0

Library of Congress Control Number: 2017958047

1 2 3 4 5 6 7 8 9 10
Written by Dr. C. Morgan Grefe
Art by Phoenix Chan
Design by Mikahla Dawson
Published by Stillwater River Publications, Glocester, RI, USA

Publisher's Cataloging-In-Publication Data
(Prepared by The Donohue Group, Inc.)

Names: Grefe, C. Morgan. | Chan, Phoenix, illustrator. | Diossa, James A., writer of
    supplementary textual content.
Title: The world in one square mile: Central Falls. / written by Dr. C. Morgan Grefe ;
    illustrated by Phoenix Chan ; foreword by Mayor James A. Diossa.
Description: First Stillwater River Publications edition. | Glocester, RI, USA : Stillwater
    River, [2017] | Interest age level: 007-012. | Summary: "An illustrated history
    of Central Falls, Rhode Island, told through the eyes of immigrant children
    from various time periods (1700, 1788, 1879, 1862, 1877, 1905, 1935, 1978,
    2006) and nationalities (indigenous, English, Irish, Polish, Syrian, Colombian,
    Cape Verdean)."--Provided by publisher.
Identifiers: ISBN 9781946300317 | ISBN 1946300314
Subjects: LCSH: Immigrant children--Rhode Island--Central Falls--History--Juvenile
    fiction. | Central Falls (R.I.)--History--Juvenile fiction. | CYAC: Immigrant child-
    ren--Rhode Island--Central Falls--History--Fiction. | Central Falls (R.I.)--
    History--Fiction.
Classification: LCC PZ7.1.G74 Ce 2017 | DDC [Fic]--dc23

The World in One Square Mile
Central Falls

Foreword by Mayor James A. Diossa

Written by Dr. C. Morgan Grefe

Illustrated by Phoenix Chan

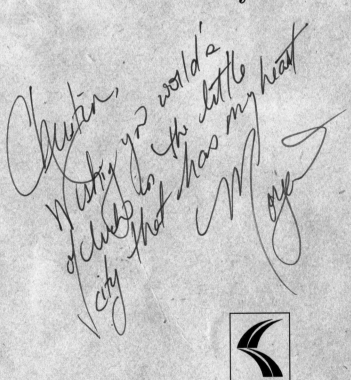

Hi! My name is James A. Diossa. I am the Mayor of Central Falls. I am a proud American of Colombian descent. My parents Bernardo and Melva came to the United States in the early 1980s in search of a better life and a future for their children. I was lucky to be born and raised in Central Falls with my two brothers and was able to see the many different traditions and customs from around the world because of our City's beautiful diversity. I attended Captain Hunt for kindergarten, Veterans Memorial for Elementary and Central Falls High School for middle school and high school and I graduated in 2003. In 2012, I became the first Latino and the youngest mayor in the history of Central Falls. In 2014 I had the privilege of meeting President Barack Obama — a man who continues to inspire me to do all that I can to make my community a better place. I hope you enjoy reading about the many people and cultures that together have made Central Falls' remarkable history.

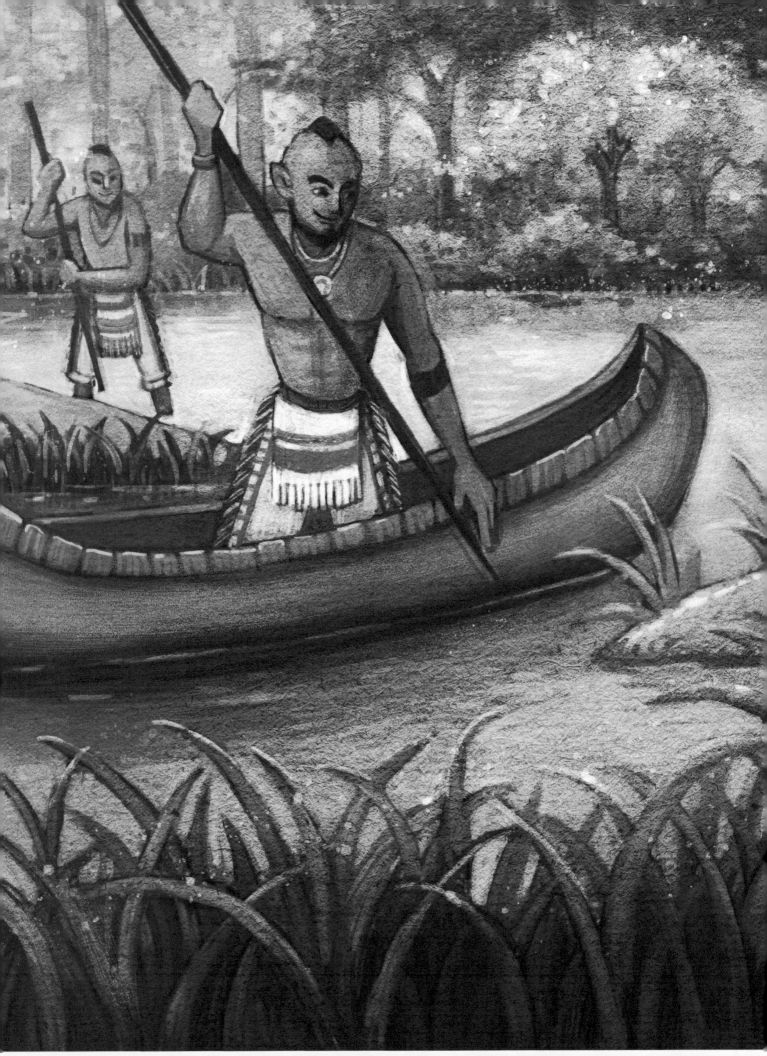

1700

What Cheer, *Netop*? This might sound like a funny greeting to you, but "What Cheer" is how the local English men and women used to ask, "How are you?" and "Netop" means friend in the language of my *Narragansett* people. By the time you read these lines, many more languages will have come to our shores, but today I want to tell you how we think of this land, this place on the falls.

We are known as the *Narragansett*, which means, "people of the small point of land." Oh, I'm so sorry, have I not told you who I am? My name is Peshauônk, which means "Flower" in my language. My friends call me Peshaw for short. Perhaps you know that from the **fine** book Mister Roger Williams wrote about our people? He called it *A Key into the Language of America*. Some people say it is a dictionary, but really, it is so much more. It is a book that told the people of England how we lived.

Our lives are shaped by this land in which we make our home. I think that is what my *Nosh* (father) and *Nokasu* (mother), would like me to share with you.

This land was formed and shaped more than 570 million years ago by a huge **glacier** that carved the land and formed the rivers. To the south is Pawtucket, a word that means, "a place of the great falls." To the west is the Moshassuck River. To the north is Valley Pond and the town that I think you now call Lincoln. To the east is what you now call the Blackstone River, named for an Englishman called William Blackstone who came here to the river valley so that he could find a quiet place to read. This river, though, is known by many names by many different peoples, from the Sneechteconnet (meaning "rocks in or along the river")

in Woonsocket to the Kittacuck ("the great tidal river") as you move closer to the bay. These are all names of this one river.

While the falls here in the middle, or the central falls, might not be as grand as the falls downstream, we do have the highest point in the city at Dexter's Ledge in Jenks Park. Or perhaps you've heard the other name for it: Quinsniket. It is 89 feet above sea level and from it you can see miles around.

We live in this area in the cold months, but for the rest of the year we live in villages on the coast. By doing this, it allows us to be closer to ponds in the winter for ice fishing and the woods for hunting. The winter is also a very social time for us. We live in longhouses in the winter with our whole families from many generations! For us, the Blackstone River is one of the most important **natural resources** in this area. It provides us with water, transportation, food, and raw materials for making items such as tools and medicines. The river is rich with fish like salmon, shad, alewives and herring. We eat some of the meat and fish right away, but the rest we must preserve to eat later when food is not as plentiful.

In the summer, when we move back to the coast, we will settle in our villages, and move into smaller wigwams, or wetus, in which we live. Unlike the winter, when we have much time to spend with our families, we are very busy outside in the spring and summer. We plant fields of corn and beans, we gather berries and nuts, and, of course there is still hunting and fishing that can be done.

And we are not alone in this land. There are many people here: the *Wampanoag* Nations such as at the *Pokanoket*, to the northeast, the *Niantic* to the southwest, and the *Nipmuc* to the north and northwest. All of our languages are similar. They are part of what is called the Algonquin Language Family—you remember, the one about which Mr. Williams wrote. Because of the ecosystems in which we live, we eat foods that are much the same

This is an artist's interpretation of Metacomet. English colonists called him King Philip. "Philip alias Metacomet of Pokanoket," Sinclair's, n.d. (RHi X17 2868)

and we lead similar lives, moving with the seasons, but we are independent peoples who live in our own communities and we have our own leaders. Yet, because the Narragansett are the largest nation in the area, most of the surrounding people pay tribute to our leaders. Some of the Massachusetts Indians are even under the domain of the Narragansett.

I hope to have the chance one day to say to you, *Wunnegin*, or welcome, and have you join us for a delicious bowl of *Nasaump*, or *Samp*, a traditional meal of corn beaten, boiled and eaten with maple syrup. Now many people eat it with milk and butter, because that is how the English prepared it. We now eat things that the colonists brought with them, but just as much, they eat foods that we introduced to them, like this delicious corn porridge. There is nothing tastier on a cold day on the Blackstone!

But this wasn't always a place for sharing meals. There have been some very sad times here by the river. *Nosh* would be disappointed in me if I did not tell you because it is a very important part of our history together.

In the 1670s, our peoples were drawn into a war because of the massacre that occurred at the Great Swamp, almost 40 miles south

of here. On March 25, 1676, Captain Michael Pierce and a company of soldiers and native scouts traveled from the Plymouth Colony to attack the Narragansett and Wampanoag settlements in Rhode Island. Crossing the Blackstone River, with a force of 64 soldiers and scouts, Pierce wanted to surprise and destroy the Narragansett settlement in Central Falls.

What Pierce did not know is that lookouts on Quinsniket had spotted them as they approached.

The Narragansett quickly moved to set up an **ambush**. Pierce believed that muskets and swords would be too much for the Narragansett warriors. But he and his men walked into a trap. The Narragansett surrounded them and waited until the colonist's **ammunition** was gone and then launched an attack. Captain Pierce was killed. Only nine of his men survived by the end of the day, and they did not live to see the next.

Even though the Narragansett won this battle, the war caused terrible loss and permanent damage to our people. After this terrible war, many of the Narragansett were sold into slavery in the Caribbean, others were displaced as far away as New York. But, many of my people stayed here in Rhode Island to make their homes, and they are still a vital and important part of their communities and of Rhode Island.

1785

Joseph is the name, how do you do? What an exciting time to be here in the colony, I mean, the state of Rhode Island! We are still at war, of course, but still our mighty Blackstone River is drawing people like my father and mother to settle here in the Great Woods of Providence.

When my grandparents came to Rhode Island from England in the 1750s, they brought with them their families, a few **possessions**, and what they had learned at home about the power of water! In fact, in 1780 our friend Charles Keene built the first **dam** to hold back the flow of the river which was located down on Roosevelt Ave. Because, did you know it's not just water that is needed, but falling water? And we certainly have that here.

And it wasn't just Mr. Keene—we made everything we needed right here in the woods. Mr. Benjamin Jenks was the first to build a waterwheel to power his **mill** in 1750. This large wheel turned a grinding stone to grind corn and tobacco into a powdered version of **snuff**. Not long after, Captain Stephen Jenks

"Pawtucket Falls in 1789," from An Illustrated History of Pawtucket, Central Falls, and Vicinity by Robert Grieve (RHi X17 2871)

built a trip hammer and blacksmith shop to **manufacture** iron hardware for use on ships. He also made tools for farming and building. And just a few years ago, in 1777, Benjamin Cozzens operated a fulling mill. Fulling is when you hit wool with a large hammer to clean and straighten it out. But, you must know that already!

Well, wheat and wool are one thing, but there is something far more wonderful being made right here by the river: chocolate! William Wheat constructed a two-story mill that would manufacture some of the first chocolate in America. Some people have even taken to calling this "Chocolateville." Wheat sells his chocolate to the military and ship owners. Many people believe that chocolate has **medicinal** properties and sea captains, sailors and soldiers often drink chocolate when they are injured or sick.

Do you ever take chocolate when you aren't feeling well? Does your chocolate come from Central Falls?

1829

I'll have to be quick, there is so much work to be done! My name is Phoebe and my family has a farm here near the Blackstone. Our neighbors used to all be farmers, too, but things are changing quickly here. It used to be that we grew and made what we needed, now we manufacture things that people all over the world need!

Because of the power of the Blackstone, small mills, factories, and shops sprang up along river's shores. Soon mill owners were competing against one another to dam the river and use the river as a source of power. Many people think we need to use waterfalls for power, but that's not how it works at all. We need to control the water, so men were needed to dig what they called "mill ponds" to hold the water and then build dams to release the water a little bit at a time. There weren't enough people here to do all of this work, so hundreds of men from Ireland moved to Rhode Island and began to do this backbreaking work. In the heat of the summer and cold chill of winter, these men had to dig and build so that the new factories could run.

Just as Samuel Slater showed the young country how to make textiles faster and cheaper using water power, the mill owners in Central Falls adapted their machinery to follow suit. Soon large mills dotted the banks of the river in Central Falls. The city grew as more and more people settled beyond the river.

Weavers, mechanics, tool makers, carpenters, textile workers, masons, coopers, tinsmiths, and farmers came to Central Falls. Stores, shops, stables, lumberyards, and coal yards opened in the village. Textile mills turned out blankets, socks, and cotton shirts.

One family you really should know about are the Wilkinsons. They are an entire family of inventors! Everyone knows their incredible mechanical devices and inventions. Oziel Wilkinson built **forges** that made anchors, nails, and screws. Have you seen their machine shop down on the river in Pawtucket? It's run by a giant waterwheel in the cellar!

And we don't make just yarn and cloth. Some 17 years ago, when the war came in 1812, the United States government desperately needed muskets. Stephen Jenks invented the machinery to quickly produce 10,000 muskets that cost $11.50 each! Quite a good price.

This is an exciting and important place to live—and I am going to write all about it! I know, it's not proper for a girl to be a writer, but my father doesn't believe in such "proper" thinking. He taught me to read and write, just like my brothers. Up in Lowell, women are working in factories and living in boarding houses with other women. Women work in mills right here in the valley. The mills are changing the world, but I know what I want to be: I want to be a teacher. My father says that when we learn, we are in control of our own destiny, and what could be more exciting than that?

"View of Falls From Cross St. Bridge," E.L. Freeman Co. postcard, n.d. (RHi X17 2850)

Workers at an unidentified foundry proudly showing their workspace, ca. 1875 (RHi X3 117)

1862

Hello there, I am Cathleen and it is a pleasure to meet you. I wanted to tell you about the place where I live. It's called Central Falls, and even though it's still pretty small, it's growing very quickly. When I was born in 1851, there were only about 1,500 people who called Central Falls home. In fact, it's not even a town yet—it's a village in a bigger town called Smithfield.

But, I have heard my parents talking about some problems with the town. Smithfield says that Central Falls is a city and the farmers in the rest of the town don't want to pay for everything in the city, like fire fighters. The farmers think it just costs too much. I don't know what will happen, but I think they are right to call us a city. With the awful war, the mills are busier and busier every day.

One of the things they need the most for the war is fabric for uniforms, blankets, and tents. In fact, my father works for the Stafford Mill right on the Blackstone River. He tells me that every day there are men and women coming to work in the factories, and they are coming from many other countries.

I was born here in Rhode Island, and so was my *Da*—that's what I call my father. But my mother was born in Ireland. She and her parents came here during the Great Famine in Ireland. All of their food just rotted in the fields and there was no work. People died of starvation. *Mam*, my mother, doesn't like to talk about it. But, they heard there was work for everyone here in Rhode Island.

Life was hard for Irish people when they came here, though. Some people didn't like the Irish, so they gave them only the worst jobs. It was hard labor, but our families worked hard and now things are getting easier.

The factories are growing so quickly. Many people are saying the mills will need to find people from other countries who can take the place of the men who will have to go off to fight in the war.

I wonder what far off place they will come from? Will they speak English like me? Personally, I can't wait to meet them!

The need for textiles kept growing, and women remained an important part of the industrial workforce throughout the 19th century, the 20th century and even today. The woman in this photograph is operating a high-speed warper, 1935 (RHi X17 2867).

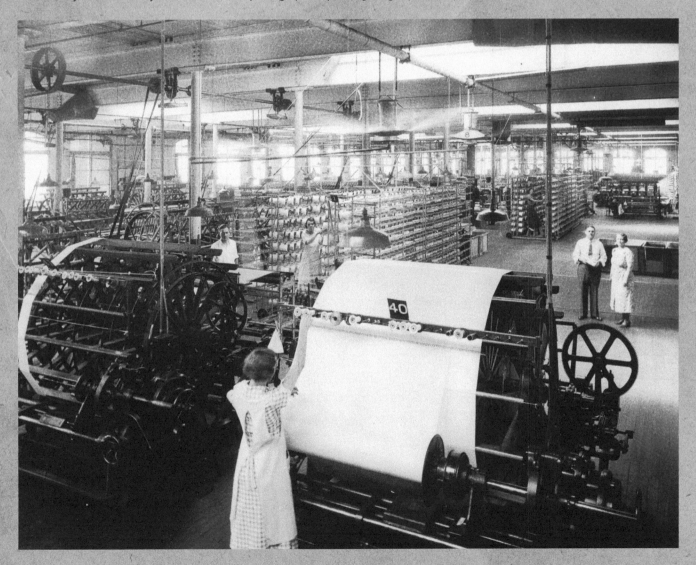

"The Dinner Hour, J. & P. Coats Thread Mill," Valentine & Sons Publishing Co. postcard, n.d. (RHi X1.7 2851)

1877

Bonjour mes amis, my name is Fabrice and I am now ten years old. I have lived in Central Falls for a long time—nearly half of my life, in fact!

I was six years old when my parents left the farm in Begin, Quebec. We had a big family there, but there was not enough work for everyone and sometimes there was not even enough food. We heard that there were places in Rhode Island where thousands of men and women made things like cloth, metal tools, and glass. Oh, yes, there are mills in Quebec's biggest city, Montreal, but they paid much less. In Montreal my father would make 55 cents a day, but in Rhode Island, he would make $1.50 in just one day!

A man, called an **agent**, came to our village and told us about these mills. It was

hard to leave our village and our family, but we knew we would have money to send home and so many of our friends were in Rhode Island already, it wouldn't be so hard to get used to.

So, we boarded a train and we traveled to our new home in Central Falls. The agent warned us that we would have to make many adjustments in Rhode Island. One of the biggest differences was that on the farm, we all worked from sun up to sundown, but in Central Falls, we worked by the clock. Can you see any clock towers on your walk to school?

Mon pere, or my father, works at the Conant Thread Mills. There are two huge, new buildings over on Rand Street. Do you know the ones I mean? They make the best thread and it is used all over the world. Maybe someone back in my village is using the thread that *mon pere* makes! It is hard work, though. The mills are so loud you can't hear anyone

"Pacific Street," Valentine & Sons Publishing Co. postcard, 1914 (RHi X17 2858)

speak, not that you are allowed to talk on the shop floor. Grease and oil from the machines get onto the floors and it becomes very slippery when you are walking around in leather-soled shoes. Many people where my parents work have been badly hurt. But, it was good work and for the first time in a long time, my parents had a lot of hope.

When we got to Central Falls, I thought I would have to work in the mills, too, but *mon pere* said I was too young for such dangerous work, so I went to the new school on Broad Street. There I would learn English like the other boys and girls, but I still spoke French at home and when I was with my friends. I think it's very special to be able to speak both. I just wish I spoke other languages so I could understand all the people here from different countries.

Every morning *Pere* gets up, drinks his coffee, and walks down Broad Street to work. We don't live too far away, and I have family living above and below me. We live in something called a **three-decker** and it's grander than any farm house I've ever seen! In fact, they call them three-deckers because way back in the old days, giant ships had three decks and people started calling all sorts of giant things "three-deckers."

I do like living in our new city house, but what I like most is that we can rent our apartment on the top floor. Our aunt and uncle own the house and live on the middle floor, and our *Meme* and *Pepe* (that's my grandmother and grandfather) live on the first floor. My parents say it's easier to be so far from home with so much of our family nearby.

"Jenks Park and Cogswell Memorial Clock Tower," Metropolitan News Co. postcard, n.d. (RHi X17 2856)

1905

Cześć, or should I say, 'hello,' my name is Jolanta and soon I will turn ten years old. Today I wanted to tell you about my favorite place in the world. It's called Jenks Park and just last year they added the most magnificent thing—a giant tower with a secret **grotto** underneath it. Don't believe me? Look at the pictures!

Right here in the new city of Central Falls (the city and I were born in the same year!) there are things being made every day: machines, tools, cloth, thread, glass. **Raw materials** arrive on trains and carts and **products** leave the same way. Every day there are new things, new people to see. It's so very exciting and there is always so much happening. You know, I heard that Rhode Island is the wealthiest state in all of the country right now. I think a lot of that has

to do with what's being made in Central Falls every day.

But sometimes it gets too busy and everyone needs to get away from the **hustle and bustle** of city life, so a man named Alvin Jenks gave the city four acres of land to turn into a beautiful park. The park has gentle hills and curved paths that we use to walk, or promenade. And there are huge iron umbrellas made by Fales & Jenks under which bands play in the summer.

While we are in the park, we visit the huge ponds filled with beautiful fish and a giant fountain on top of the hill. A big, beautiful elk statue stands on a giant, ancient boulder. My mother tells me that there were parks just like this in the city near where she grew up in Poland. She takes me for walks in Jenks Park when she is home from the mill and tells me about my *babciu* and *dziadek*, that's grandmother and grandfather in Polish. She misses her home in Poland, but she says that here in Rhode Island, she can make a better life for me and my five brothers and sisters.

In the middle of the park is a high cliff called Dexter's Ledge. A couple of years ago they started building a huge stone tower on top of it. The tower is a present from Mrs. Caroline Cogswell, who used to live here before she moved to California. The tower is nearly 70 feet tall and has a clock on each of its four sides. Under each clock is an iron railing and an observation deck. You can go out on the deck and see all of Central Falls, the river, Pawtucket, and even Lincoln.

People from all over come to Central Falls to see our beautiful park and tower. There is no better place to see your neighbors and appreciate how wonderful our new city is.

"Scene in Jenks Park," Oscar's Variety Store postcard, n.d. (RHi X17 2847)

"Jenks Park," Robbins Bros. Co. postcard, n.d. (RHi X17 2846)

1935

Line of employees waiting in the snow outside Sayles Finishing Plants, Inc., ca. 1924 (RHi S275 677)

Marhaban, **my friends.** I am Saad and though you may not know it, I was saying hello to you in my family's native language of Arabic. Even though I was born here in Central Falls, my parents and grandparents came here from Syria in 1911. They were not able to bring very much with them, but one thing that they shared with me was our language. So now at 10 years old I am able to speak not only Arabic and English, but even a little Portuguese, French and Polish so that I can say hello to my friends' parents when I visit them!

We live right in the center of town on Pacific Street, so it is very easy for all of us to walk to work. Things have been hard with the closing of so many of the textile mills. My father is a **tailor**, which means that he makes and fixes clothes for people. My mother also helps in the shop and is a wonderful **seamstress** and can make any type of dress any lady might want. When people are out of work, though, they aren't getting many new clothes made, so business has been slow.

It's not just that money has been tight, it's been downright scary here. Last year on **Labor Day** over in Saylesville, the workers went out on strike and Governor T.F. Green called in the state police and even wanted to arm war veterans and call in Federal troops! The National Guard came in and fired on the workers, who were fighting back with their fists. The fighting lasted for three weeks and even spread to cities like Woonsocket. Hundreds of people were hurt and a few were killed. If you go over to the Moshassuck Cemetery you can even see bullet holes in the grave stones. It was a terrible time.

Still, I like living right near the center of town because that's where all of the action is. There are shops up and down Broad Street where you can get anything you've ever wanted. Jenks Park is so beautiful in the spring and I like to go up to the Cogswell Tower to pretend I'm a look out like in the old days.

Did you hear that just a few years back the city built the most beautiful high school? I can't wait to go there. It's yellow brick and it looks like one of those Greek temples I saw in a book over at the Adams Library on Central Street. Do you go there? My *Baba* (that's what we call my father) tells me that before the library was built, all of the books were kept in the old fire house. We have some of the best buildings in Rhode Island, such as the library and the police station at 505 Broad Street.

What do you think are the most beautiful buildings in Central Falls?

My favorite is the grand Pawtucket-Central Falls train station. I never get tired of going down to watch the trains and all of the bustle of businessmen coming and going. Sometimes I imagine being one of them running through the gigantic lobby to make my way to my train bound for New York City!

Even with the hard times, my *Baba* always says, "This is a city on the move!"

LIVE
AND LET LIVE!

We, the help of Hope, Jackson, Fiskville, Arkwright, Harrisville, and Lippitt Mills, have

Resolved, That we will not resume our work in the above mentioned Mills unless our employers will pay us the same wages as we had before the reduction of our wages in 1857; and we hereby solicit the sympathy of all in our cause.

We furthermore request all other operatives not to interfere with our cause by taking our places at lower wages than we now ask for. We believe that the Manufacturers can afford to pay us all that we ask for, as we make nothing but a reasonable demand.

Any one desirous of further information upon this subject, is invited to attend our meetings, the next of which will be holden in the

Harrisville Grove,

On MONDAY, May 24, at 10 o'clock, A. M.

By order of the Committee.

May 21st, 1858.

...n ye that ye beat my people to pieces,
...e faces of the poor? saith the Lord
...----Isa. iii: 15.

Strikes were nothing new in Rhode Island. This is a broadside, sort of like a poster, in which workers are threatening a strike in 1858 (RHi X4 129).

1978

Just about 10 years ago my father came to Central Falls. My mother, brother and I stayed back in Barranquilla, Colombia. I had just been born, so it would have been very hard for us to leave our home. Plus, the only job there was for my father, in the huge Pontiac Mill.

I know everybody thinks their dad is a hero, but mine really is a superhero. Back in Colombia he worked as a loom fixer in a huge textile mill. You might not know this, but down in Colombia, there are as many mills as there are up here! Anyway, it turns out that in the 1960s, the mill owners up here were having a hard time finding people who knew how to fix their machines—it's a very complicated job. But my *padre*, he managed seven looms and could fix them faster than anyone. Just like when they went to Quebec years ago, agents from Rhode Island went down to places like Barranquilla and Medellin, Colombia to recruit the best workers. One day a man came to my father in the factory and said that he wanted him to come up to Rhode Island for a job. At first, *Papi* said "No way, there's too much snow up there! It's too cold." But my *mami*, she said, "Oh yes, you're taking that job. Your mother is still working. She's too old for this and soon we will have another mouth to feed."

So up he came, but he thought he would be coming back in a few years. Since he didn't plan to stay, he lived in an apartment with a few other workers who had come up from Colombia. He worked as many shifts

The Blizzard of 1978; Image courtesy of James Such.

as he could, managing up to 100 looms at a time! Just so he could send all of his money home to us.

For a couple of years, other than the Colombians he worked with, there were very few people in Central Falls who spoke Spanish. There were only two Spanish markets to get food—and they were all the way in Providence!

He was so lonely, but the money was good, and the mills needed more and more workers, so he knew the loneliness would only be temporary. Soon my aunts, uncles and our friends were moving up and just a few years ago, we were all able to come here.

I was so happy to see my *papi* again, and he was glad to see me, his little Consuela... but it is cold! One day in a snowstorm he had to walk what seemed like 20 blocks (even though our city is only one square mile!) home from work because the buses weren't running. By the time he got home he had icicles hanging off his mustache!

And you know what, in just ten years, so much has changed. Lots of kids in my school speak Spanish, and even a couple of the teachers do, too. Do you know anyone who speaks Spanish?

I bet by the time you read this, many more people will have come up from Colombia, because my *papi* says that the factories will always need smart workers. Are people still coming to Central Falls from Colombia? Where is your family from?

2006

My name is Maria Julia and I come from a small country made up of several islands off the coast of West Africa called Cabo Verde, or Cape Verde. I've not been in Central Falls very long, but I want to tell you why I am so very glad to be here. This country, this city, is so very wonderful. When we left our home, my parents were looking for better job opportunities for themselves and a better education for me. My parents were trying for many years to get us out and to find a place to make a new home, and the United States allowed us to come here. It's been so exciting!

When we were preparing for our journey, we learned about Rhode Island from those who had already come here and they told us that this place had a great history of ancestors from Cape Verde who came looking for opportunities just like us. I might only be 10 years old, but I already know what opportunity means and this seems like a good story to be a part of.

Many others from our country went to places like Brockton and Boston, Massachusetts, but there are thousands of us right here in Central Falls and Pawtucket. It reminds us of home in so many ways, but mostly it's because we can live so close to our friends and relatives. We don't have to travel for hours to see everyone. We can be almost anywhere we need to be in 10 minutes! And there are groups of people from Cape Verde already here who helped us when we arrived, so we had friends immediately.

One of the things my parents worried about while we were in Cape Verde was my education. In Cape Verde, the school was so far away from my town and it was often difficult to get to. My *Mai* and *Pai* (my mom and dad, that is) want me to go to school and

Formerly a community eyesore, this property located at 115 Illinois Street, which is adjacent to the Central Falls High School, has been reborn as the McKenna Center for Teaching, Learning and Research.

study hard so that I can become a doctor or a lawyer! In Central Falls, the schools are close by and I get to go to school every day. My father takes classes at night to learn English, too.

One of my favorite things to do back in Cape Verde was watching my uncles play uril, a marble game that comes from West Africa. I'd also play soccer with my friends. I am happy because I can do both here. Can you believe that some of my friends that live on my street are Cape Verdean, too? I play soccer with them almost every day on Watson St. It's fun because they also speak Creole. We practice our Creole with each other because our parents say that it's important not to lose our culture, even though we are proud to be Americans.

Cape Verdeans also enjoy the card game of Bezique. This card game is typically played at family gatherings, barbecues or even before we sit down to watch a football game. If you've never played, I think you'd really like it. I've heard other people say it's very similar to another card game called pinochle.

I love it here in Central Falls, but I do miss some of the food from home. In my town we would cook traditional foods like cachupa, canja, and pastels. Maybe when I grow up I can open my own restaurant and make our traditional Cape Verdean dishes for you and your family. What foods remind you of home? I'd love to try them.

Something else I like to do is look at all the houses and buildings in the city. Some of them look so old. I often wonder who used to live in them. For example, my house is over 100 years old! I found newspapers in the basement and they were in all sorts of languages. I recognized some of the French and Portuguese words, but I don't know the other ones. Do you know who used to live in your house?

Formerly the site of an abandoned and dilapidated VFW building, 416 Hunt Street has been revitalized and is now the home of Veterans Memorial Park.

A favorite Cape Verdean pastime is the annual New Year's celebration of *Canta-reis,* when folks go from home to home on New Year's day. At each home they visit, the host offers either food or an official New Year's toast and maybe even joins those already gathered to visit the next home on the list. The celebrations typically end with a large supper at the home of the last person they visit.

A family member told me an old practice from the 1940s and 50s involving the sere-nading of women by potential suitors on Cape Verde. These young men would go to the windows of the young ladies they were interested in and serenade them. I wonder what songs we would sing today.

If you get to attend a barbecue at the home of a Cape Verdean family, "beanies, weenies and sliders" would be the side dish. And you can expect some rice-based dish, chourico, linguica or cachupa to be part of the fare. Just a hint: It is also customary to bring beverages and a dish or dessert, even if not asked to. But you better be hungry, there's going to be a lot of food. We'll be waiting for you with a full plate!

The historic Cogswell Tower, located at Jenks Park, as it looks in 2018.

And Today ... What's your story?

Glossary

Agent: a person who acts on behalf of another, in particular a business or company.

Ambush: a surprise attack by people lying in wait in a concealed position.

Ammunition: a supply or quantity of bullets.

Dam: a barrier constructed to hold back water and raise its level, the resulting pond being used in the production of electricity or as a water supply.

Forge: a blacksmith's workshop where he/she makes things out of iron and steel.

Glacier: a slowly moving mass or river of ice formed by the accumulation and compaction of snow on mountains or near the poles.

Grotto: a small picturesque cave, especially an artificial one in a park or garden.

Hustle and bustle: A large amount of activity and work, usually in a noisy and busy area.

Labor Day: a public holiday or day of festivities held in honor of working people, or laborers, in the U.S. and Canada on the first Monday in September, in many other countries on May 1.

Manufacture: the making of objects on a large scale using machinery.

Medicinal: something that has healing properties.

Mill: a building equipped with machinery.

Natural resource: materials or substances such as minerals, forests, water, and fertile land that occur in nature and can be used for economic gain.

Possessions: an item of property; something belonging to someone.

Product: something that is made for sale.

Raw material: the basic matter or things from which a product is made.

Seamstress: a woman who sews, especially one who earns her living by sewing.

Snuff: powdered tobacco that is sniffed up the nostril rather than smoked.

Tailor: a person whose job is making fitted clothes such as suits, pants, and jackets to fit individual customers.

Three-decker: A three-story apartment building, also called a triple-decker in the U.S.; these buildings are typically made out of wood and each floor usually has one apartment.

Acknowledgments

This book was written with tremendous and invaluable help from many members of our Rhode Island community. Each person brought their unique skill set, talents, and enthusiasm to this project and made it even more of a joy to pull together. There are so many more people to thank, but here are just a few whose words and wisdom helped shape *The World in One Square Mile: Central Falls*.

For help with content we turned to the Executive Director of the Tomaquag Museum, Lorén Spears; Anna Cano-Morales, Associate Vice President for Community, Equity and Diversity for Rhode Island College; Central Falls High School social studies teacher and font of Central Falls historical knowledge Robert Scappini; Central Falls historian Thomas Shannahan; Chief Joyce Eaglecries Gauvin, who lent her expertise in both content and elementary school education; Victoria Pendragon, who assisted with readability and internal consistencies; and Marie Parys, co-director of National History Day in Rhode Island, former social studies teacher and librarian, and an integral part of the Rhode Island Historical Society team!

We would like to especially thank Denise Debarros and the Cape Verdean Student Association at Central Falls High School, who created the section on the Cape Verdean experience (pages 40-41).

There were also a number of people at the Rhode Island Historical Society who helped out with their areas of expertise and access: Ann Dionne and Shawn Badgley helped on copy editing, Geralyn Ducady helped with content and readability, intern Erin Perfect assembled Central Falls images, and Henry Sanchez was an incredible photo finder. We must give a huge thanks to J.D. Kay, the RIHS imaging specialist who prepared an extraordinary number of images from the RIHS collection for our use in this book – it would be a far less beautiful project without them!

We would also like to thank members of Mayor Diossa's administrative team, Joshua Giraldo and Derek Collamati, for all of their work in helping bring this book to fruition.

And, of course, none of this work would be possible without the generous support of the Rhode Island Foundation, a community organization dedicated to supporting good work right here in our backyard!

Thank you all!